Life on the Edge

Living in DESERTS

Tea Benduhn

Reading consultant: Susan Nations, M.Ed., author/literacy coach/
consultant in literacy development

WEEKLY READER
PUBLISHING

Please visit our web site at: **www.garethstevens.com**
For a free color catalog describing our list of high-quality books,
call 1-800-542-2595 (USA) or 1-800-387-3178 (Canada).

Library of Congress Cataloging-in-Publication Data

Benduhn, Tea.
    Living in deserts / Tea Benduhn.
       p. cm. — (Life on the edge)
    ISBN-10: 0-8368-8741-1 (lib. hdg.)
    ISBN-13: 978-0-8368-8741-1 (lib. hdg.)
    ISBN-10: 0-8368-8916-1 (softcover)
    ISBN-13: 978-0-8368-8346-6 (softcover)
    1. Deserts—Juvenile literature.   2. Human geography—
Juvenile literature. I. Title.
  GF55.B46   2008
  910.915'4—dc22   2007014748

This edition first published in 2008 by
Weekly Reader® Books
An imprint of Gareth Stevens Publishing
1 Reader's Digest Road
Pleasantville, NY 10570-7000 USA

Copyright © 2008 by Gareth Stevens, Inc.

Managing editor: Mark Sachner
Art direction: Tammy West
Picture research: Sabrina Crewe
Production: Jessica Yanke

Picture credits: cover, title page Bobby Model/Digital Railroad; p. 5 © Lawrence Manning/Corbis; pp. 6,
19 Scott Krall/© Gareth Stevens, Inc.; p. 7 Maria Stenzel/National Geographic/Getty Images; p. 9 © Dean
Conger/Corbis; p. 10 Torsten Blackwood/AFP/Getty Images; p. 11 © Jose Fuste Raga/Corbis; p. 13 © Mark
Karrass/Corbis; p. 14 Panapress/Getty Images; p. 15 © Kazuyoshi Nomachi/Corbis; p. 16 © Liang Zhuoming/
Corbis; p. 17 © Guenter Rossenbach/Zefa/Corbis; p. 20 Charles Bowman/Robert Harding World Imagery/
Getty Images; p. 21 Frederic J. Brown/AFP/Getty Images.

Printed in the United States of America

1 2 3 4 5 6 7 8 9 11 10 09 08 07

TABLE OF CONTENTS

Cover and title page: Many people living in deserts use camels.

CHAPTER *1*

Welcome to the Desert

The air is hot and dry. Sand blows in your face. Rocks and sand are all you can see for miles and miles. You are thirsty. You will not have much luck finding water because rain has not fallen here for more than a year. Where are you? You are in a desert!

A desert is an **extreme** place to live. No other place on Earth is as dry as a desert. Fewer than 10 inches (25 centimeters) of rain fall in deserts each year. The soil is dry, and rainfall can cause a **flash flood**. In the world's deserts, more people have drowned in desert rainstorms than have died from thirst.

Flash floods happen when a desert's dry ground cannot soak up water quickly.

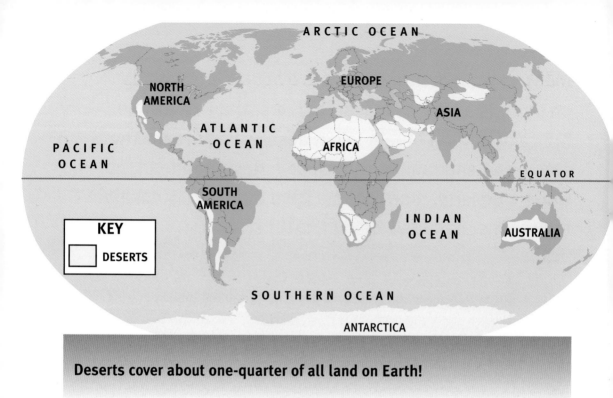

Deserts cover about one-quarter of all land on Earth!

Deserts are almost everywhere in the world. You can find deserts in South America, North America, Asia, Australia, Africa, and Antarctica.

Many deserts are hot. There are not enough clouds to shield the ground from the Sun's heat. One of the hottest temperatures ever recorded was in Death Valley, California. The temperature reached 132° Fahrenheit (56° Celsius)! Not all deserts are hot, however. Most of Antarctica is a cold desert. Temperatures there can be as low as −128° F (−89° C). That is way below freezing!

One of the coldest places on Earth, Antarctica, is a desert!

CHAPTER 2

People of the Desert

Deserts can be filled with danger. People can get **heatstroke** from extreme temperatures. Lack of water can lead to **dehydration**. Too much exposure to the Sun can cause sunburn. Some people, however, are able to live in deserts. To them, deserts are home.

For hundreds of years, people have found ways to **protect** themselves against the extreme **conditions** of deserts. They build shelters for shade during the day. They travel at night. The nomadic people of Asia's Gobi Desert move from place to place to find **resources**. They live in tent-like structures called yurts, which they carry with them.

A yurt is easy to put up, take down, and move. It will stay standing even in winds of 90 miles (145 kilometers) per hour.

Miners in Coober Pedy, on the edge of Australia's Great Victoria Desert, escape the Sun's heat in their underground homes. The town's name means "white man in a hole."

Different groups of people live in deserts around the world. Each group has its own way of life. They build different types of shelters to suit their ways of life. Some build homes with bricks they make from mixing mud with straw. Some people live underground! The people of Coober Pedy, Australia, dig underground rooms to make their homes.

Long ago, the only people who lived in deserts lived **traditional** lifestyles. Today, many kinds of people live in deserts. They use modern technology to build air-conditioned buildings and to pump water into their cities. Las Vegas, Nevada, for example, is in the Mojave Desert.

Some modern cities, such as Las Vegas, are in the middle of deserts.

CHAPTER 3

Living in the Desert

Harsh weather and **climate** make it hard for people to live in deserts. Over many years, people have learned ways to find enough water to survive. The San people of the Kalahari Desert, in Africa, for example, know which plants store water. They also use long **reeds** to suck up water from underground. They then store the water in ostrich eggshells.

Dates grow on palm trees. People can eat them or trade them for money or other goods.

Most people who live in deserts live near an **oasis**. An oasis has enough water to grow crops. Many people have palm trees. A fruit called a date grows on these trees. People can also grow olive trees, wheat, and other crops for food. If an oasis is big enough, people can build villages, towns, or even cities around it.

These Tuareg people live in the Sahara Desert. They cover their faces with long, flowing cloaks. Their clothes keep sand out of their eyes, hair, mouths, and skin.

Very few plants grow in deserts. Often, deserts go on for hundreds of miles of land with no shade. Strong winds blow through the **barren** landscape. A dust storm can strike at any moment without warning. Desert people wear layers of loose-fitting clothes to protect themselves from the Sun and blowing dust.

Some people who live in deserts do not stay in one place. The Tuareg people live in the Sahara Desert in Africa. For hundreds of years, they have traveled across the desert. They carried items for trade, such as gold and spices, from one side of the desert to the other.

The Tuareg people raise goats to provide milk and meat and to carry water across the desert.

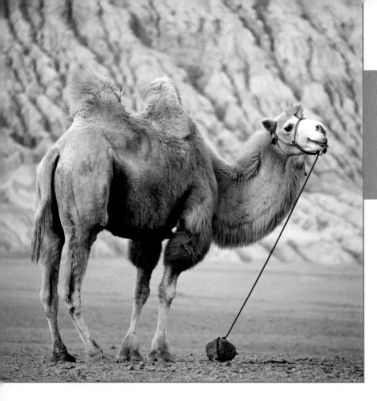

Camels have often been called "ships of the desert." They can live for a long time off the fat stored in their humps.

For hundreds of years, many people have used camels to travel through the desert. Camels are built to survive desert weather and climate. Their thick, wooly hair protects them from the hot Sun. Their wide feet stop them from sinking in the sand. They can drink 25 gallons (95 liters) of water in minutes, and they do not need to drink again for days.

Fewer than one hundred years ago, many people could not cross a desert without a camel. Today, camels are less important than they once were. People now drive cars and trucks through deserts. Deserts are easier to cross today, but you would not want to get stranded! You may not get help for a long time.

Strong winds blow sand through deserts. Blowing sand makes it hard for drivers to see the road.

CHAPTER 4

People and the Desert Today

Every year, more people live on the edges of deserts. They cut down trees for fuel and farm the land. They bring animals, such as goats, to **graze** on the land. The areas surrounding deserts cannot support all the people who live in them. Humans use up lots of water. As people use the land, the soil loses its **nutrients** and becomes weak.

Most kinds of plants cannot grow in weak soil. Without plants to hold the soil in place, it can dry out and blow away in heavy winds. Dry earth can cover smaller plants and stop them from growing. Every year, more land turns into desert, and the world's deserts grow bigger. The spreading of desert edges is called **desertification**.

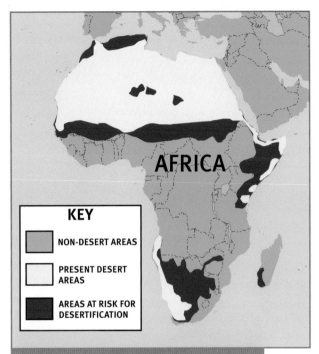

KEY

NON-DESERT AREAS

PRESENT DESERT AREAS

AREAS AT RISK FOR DESERTIFICATION

AFRICA

The yellow areas on this map show the current desert areas in Africa. The red shows areas at risk for desertification.

Desert mines cause pollution that can spread to other parts of the world.

Some people harm deserts. They have found valuable resources in the desert. Large companies mine deserts for precious metals, such as gold. Others drill for oil. Some nations test bombs and other weapons in deserts. Such use of deserts causes **pollution**, which can spread to the rest of the world. Pollution of the desert can harm the whole planet.

Some people, however, are trying to save deserts. **Conservation** scientists are trying to replant areas that have become desert. They build plastic covers over healthy crops, which stops plants from drying out. Some governments restrict the ways people can use the land. Other deserts are protected as national parks. Protecting deserts can help the planet.

Scientists hope to stop the spread of deserts by planting new crops and trees. They cover the plants with plastic covers that look like tunnels.

Glossary

barren — not able to have living things grow

climate — the weather and temperature usually found in an area

conservation — having to do with careful protection of something

dehydration — extreme thirst or the state of being without enough body fluids due to lack of water

desertification — the changing of fertile land into desert

extreme — having more of something, such as heat or dryness, than we are used to

flash flood – a sudden, violent flood that occurs in heavy rainstorms

graze – feed on grass

heatstroke – extremely high body temperature as a result of too much exposure to the Sun

nutrients – substances that living things need to grow

oasis – a place in a desert that has water

pollution – human-made waste that harms the environment

protect – keep safe

reeds – tall grasses with long, stiff stems

resources – natural substances that people can use to make their lives better

traditional – having to do with a way of life and beliefs that have been in use for many generations

For More Information

Books

Deserts. Habitats (series). Fran Howard (Buddy Books)

Deserts. Heinemann First Library (series). Angela Royston (Heinemann)

Deserts. Learning About the Earth (series). Emily K. Green (Bellwether Media)

Deserts. Where on Earth? (series). JoAnn Early Macken (Gareth Stevens)

Web Sites

Biomes of the World: Deserts

www.mbgnet.net/sets/desert/index.htm

Click on the links to find out more about deserts.

Desert Sandbox

www.dpcinc.org/kids.shtml

Click on the links to play desert games and more.

Publisher's note to educators and parents: Our editors have carefully reviewed these Web sites to ensure that they are suitable for children. Many Web sites change frequently, however, and we cannot guarantee that a site's future contents will continue to meet our high standards of quality and educational value. Be advised that children should be closely supervised whenever they access the Internet.

Index

About the Author

Tea Benduhn writes and edits books for children and teens. She lives in the beautiful state of Wisconsin with her husband and two cats. The walls of their home are lined with bookshelves filled with books. Tea says, "I read every day. It is more fun than watching television!"